LOUIS VUITTON

THE FASHION ICONS

sona BOOKS

© Danann Publishing Limited 2024

First Published Danann Media Publishing Limited 2024
WARNING: For private domestic use only, any unauthorised Copying, hiring, lending or public performance of this book is illegal.

CAT NO: SON0607

Photography courtesy of

Getty images:

Pierre Verdy/AFP	Fernanda Calfat	Andreas Rentz
Roger Viollet Collection	Stephane Cardinale/Corbis	Edward Berthelot
Apic	Rose Hartman/Archive Photos	Jacopo Raule
Antonio de Moraes Barros Filho	James Andanson/Sygma	George Chinsee/WWD/Penske Media
Michel Dufour/WireImage	Ray Tang/Anadolu Agency	Aurelien Meunier
Marc Piasecki/FilmMagic	Tom King/Mirrorpix	Gotham/GC Images
Francois Guillot/AFP	Raymond Hall/GC	Giovanni Giannoni/Penske Media
Pascal Le Segretain	Peter White	Billy H.C. Kwok
Petroff/Dufour	Gou Yige/AFP	Dominik Bindl
Bertrand Rindoff Petroff	David M. Benett	Victor Virgile/Gamma-Rapho
Dominique Charriau/WireImage	PIERRE GUILLAUD/AFP	Stephane De Sakutin/POOL/AFP

Alamy:

DPA Picture Alliance	The Photo Access
Abaca Press	Jeremy Sutton-Hibbert
Helen	Retro AdArchives
Sipa US	Everett Collection Inc
WENN Rights Ltd	Associated Press

Other images Wiki Commons

Cover design Darren Grice
Book design Kate Cerpnjak
Proof reader Juliette O'Neill

All rights reserved. No Part of this title may be reproduced or transmitted in any material form (including photocopying or storing it in any medium by electronic means and whether or not transiently or incidentally to some other use of this publication) without the written permission of the copyright owner, except in accordance with the provisions of the Copyright, Designs and Patents Act 1988. Applications for the copyright owner's written permission should be addressed to the publisher.

This is an independent publication and it is unofficial and unauthorised and as such has no connection with Louis Vuitton or any other organisation connected in any way whatsoever with Louis Vuitton featured in the book.

Made in EU.

ISBN: 978-1-915343-73-4

CONTENTS

INTRODUCTION 8
FROM RURAL ANCHAY TO ARISTOCRATIC PARIS 10
LOUIS VUITTON LUXURY LEATHERS 14
BY GEORGES! 18
LV BAG LADIES 28
GASTON-LOUIS 34
THE TOP TEN 42
1970 – 1997 46
HAPPY HUNDREDTH! 50
THE MARC JACOBS YEARS 54
LV BY NUMBERS 78
ST NICOLAS 80
ONLY AT LOUIS VUITTON 114
LOUIS VUITTON AND THE A LISTERS 118
SAY WHAT? 136

INTRODUCTION

'Louis Vuitton, the world's biggest luxury brand in terms of sales, is planning to dampen its expansion worldwide and focus on high-end products to preserve its exclusive image' Bernard Arnault, founder, chairman and CEO of LVMH, the world's largest luxury goods company.

In the high-altitude world of high-fashion there is exclusive, there is very exclusive and then… there is Louis Vuitton – the world's most recognised, most valuable luxury brand. Think LV and think uber luxurious leather goods, legendary steamer trunks, iconic monogram handbags, sublime watches and jewellery, and cutting-edge fashion. A Louis Vuitton original never compromises on quality, be it a watch, handbag, wallet or any other product. LV items are created with as much care and attention as they were back in 1854 when the company was founded by the original Louis Vuitton, a one-time runaway teen from the mountainous Jura region of France. Goods are never offered on sale in order to retain their cachet and exclusivity while the Maison takes vigorous legal action against forgeries. Louis Vuitton's 'LV' monogram has become synonymous with luxury, aspiration, and exclusivity, symbolizing power and affluence, elegance and creativity. Louis Vuitton and the cultural values the brand embodies blend tradition with innovation, and kindles dreams and fantasies.

THE FASHION ICONS   LOUIS VUITTON

FROM RURAL ANCHAY TO ARISTOCRATIC PARIS

'Securely packs the most fragile objects. Specializing in packing fashions'

The sign outside Louis Vuitton's first shop in Paris, circa 1854.

Louis Vuitton was born on August 4 1821 in Anchay, a small remote village in the mountainous region of eastern France known as the Jura. He hailed from a working-class family - father, Xavier Vuitton, was a farmer while his mother, Coronne Gaillard, was a milliner. Following his mother's premature death when Louis was just 10-years-old, his father remarried. By all accounts the youngster did not get along with his stepmother and was intent on leaving for the capital to escape both her and the boredom of country life. In 1835, at the tender age of 14, Louis Vuitton left home and began the 292-mile journey to Paris, becoming a journeyman/worker on the way. Travelling by foot, it took teenage Louis two years to get there.

Upon his arrival in the French capital in 1837, Louis began an apprenticeship under Monsieur Maréchal – a respected box-maker and packer located in the prestigious and tres chic Rue Saint-Honoré. At the time, 'malletiers' (which translates directly as 'trunk-makers' in English) were responsible not only for crafting luggage, but also packing and ensuring

ABOVE: Louis Vuitton
RIGHT TOP: Empress Eugénie de Montijo
RIGHT BOTTOM: Rue Neuve-des-capucines, 1852

FROM RURAL ANCHAY TO ARISTOCRATIC PARIS

the protection of their owners' valuable belongings. As it was customary to travel by horse-drawn carriages, steamboats and trains, suitcases were handled quite roughly, and thus it was no easy feat to keep valuables and elaborate garments in pristine condition. After Louis Vuitton was hired by Empress Eugénie de Montijo, the wife of Napoleon Bonaparte III, he gained a reputation as a master of the 'malletier' craft and became the Empress' personal packer. Such prestigious patronage was priceless and, as a result, the well-to-do clamoured for his services.

In 1854, Louis opened his own workshop, located at the now-historic 4 Rue Neuve-des-Capucines, close to the Place Vendôme. The sign outside read: 'Securely packs the most fragile objects. Specializing in packing fashions'. It was a busy year for him as that April he married 17-year-old Clemence-Emilie Parriaux, the daughter of a mill owner. Within four years of opening his shop, Louis had developed a stackable, waterproof trunk – regarded today as the birth of modern luggage. Instead of covering his wooden trunks in heavy, traditional pigskin, Louis upholstered them in a treated light-grey coloured canvas which was waterproof and would become

known as the 'Trianon'. The Vuitton trunks also deviated from the traditional in that the lids were flat rather than dome-shaped, making them stackable. So successful were they that before long, Vuitton's competitors were copying the design. In response, he customised his products even further by adding nailed slats of beechwood to the trunks, making them stronger and also more stylish.

In 1859, Vuitton expanded his workshop and HQ to a property in Asnières, (now known as Asnières-sur-Seine), a village some 20 miles northwest of Paris. Its location on the River Seine and near a railway line allowed for convenient river and rail transport of finished products as well as the delivery of raw materials. Asnières supplied Vuitton's city store while also providing a home for his family and a new headquarters for the business. With the rapid growth of both rail and sea travel for leisure, Louis Vuitton luggage became more sought after than ever. In 1867, he was awarded a bronze medal for his designs at the Exposition Universelle in Paris. Due to his association with Empress Eugénie, his work became known amongst the great and the good – both at home and abroad. By the end of the 1860s, he counted the likes of the Khedive of Egypt and other world heads of state as satisfied customers, with the Khedive commissioning hunting trunks, picnic trunks and even an ice box trunk.

In July 1870, France and Prussia went to war with the result that Napoleon III was deposed and the Second Empire ceased to exist. The company suffered several setbacks during the war which had paralysed travel and consequently lessened the demand for luggage. Moreover, the workshop in Asnières was ransacked, and its equipment was stolen or destroyed. After the war, however, Vuitton re-established his business and opened a new shop in Paris at 1 Rue Scribe, a prestigious location close to the Palais Garnier and the Louvre. Today the former residence at Asnières is a museum and the rest of the estate still functions as a workshop – where 170 craftsmen fulfil special orders from the brand's most VIP customers.

By the 1870s, Vuitton's son Georges, born in 1857, had joined the family business. Vuitton and son continued to experiment with new signature canvases, debuting a patterned canvas of red and beige stripes in 1872, followed by a striped canvas in beige and brown (1876) and then, in 1888, the iconic Damier design, featuring a checkerboard pattern of red and white,

ABOVE: Exposition Universelle, Paris 1867
RIGHT TOP: The iconic Damier design
RIGHT BOTTOM: Louis with son and employees, 1890

and beige and brown. To curb imitations of his work, he also stamped a brand identification on his trunks that read: marque L. Vuitton déposée (registered L. Vuitton brand).

Vuitton expanded his business outside of France in 1885 when a shop was opened on London's Oxford Street. The following year, he and Georges Vuitton developed the tumbler lock, which featured a single lock system with two spring buckles and was eventually patented by the company. Georges Vuitton was so confident in the lock's security that he is said to have challenged American magician Harry Houdini to escape from a locked Vuitton trunk. The showman, however, did not take up the challenge. Three years later, Louis Vuitton won the prestigious gold medal and grand prize at the Exposition Universelle in Paris for his brown and beige Damier design. The undisputed trunk-master, or 'malletier' of Paris, continued to work at the company he had created until he passed away from a brain tumour, aged 70, on February 27 1892.

THE FASHION ICONS   LOUIS VUITTON

LOUIS VUITTON LUXURY LEATHERS

T he House of Vuitton has an untouchable reputation in the fashion world for using only the very best textiles and leather, and developing an unrivalled répertoire of handbags and accessories in various colours, materials, finishes, prints, and quilting designs. Here are some of the classics...

COATED CANVAS

A blend of cotton and linen with a layer of cotton canvas coated with PVC for extra durability and smoothness – coated canvas is durable, water resistant and travels perfectly. Coated canvas is used to make many of Louis Vuitton's iconic bags, like the Neverfull and Speedy. The fabric comes in many different patterns and prints.

* Classic Monogram print in brown with Louis Vuitton pattern – also comes in a grey shade.

* Created in 2002 and a collaboration between Louis Vuitton and Japanese artist Takashi Murakami, the Multicolour Monogram was a many-hued version of the classic LV monogram. It is now discontinued.

* The Damiers... Ébène – the darker brown checkered pattern; Azur – the white checkered pattern; Graphite – the black and dark grey checkered pattern.

* Limited edition canvas prints – such as Cherries – are introduced seasonally.

LOUIS VUITTON LUXURY LEATHERS

EPI LEATHER

Epi leather was initially inspired by Vuitton's textured leather from the 1920s. The brand started using the fabric in 1985 - its durability, unique feel, ability to look good in any colour, ability to withstand scratches and water-resistant qualities making it a firm favourite. Epi leather is made with grained cowhide, tanned with plant extracts before the deep-dyeing process.

EMPREINTE LEATHER

Easy to maintain and clean, Empreinte leather is supple and soft yet durable. Therefore, perfect for an everyday bag. Released in 2010, Vuitton's Empreinte is embossed with the iconic LV monogram, quatrefoil and flower symbols. The embossed areas often feature contrasting colours to the main body of the bag.

EXOTIC LEATHERS

Exotic and unique yet durable – but somewhat controversial, Vuitton items made from lizard, crocodile, ostrich, and python skins are a rarity in the label's canon of work and therefore expensive in the extreme. The skins require specialist treatment to prevent 'dry-out' once crafted into bags.

LAMBSKIN

The best quality lambskin leather is used for Vuitton's luxuriously quilted and embossed handbags such as the Coussin. Finely grained, smooth and shinily soft to the touch.

CALFSKIN

Durable, versatile calfskin is an instant go-to at Louis Vuitton for handbags and small leather goods. It is a classic which requires little processing. Sleek, smooth and sophisticated yet simple-to-clean and scuff-resistant, the leather boasts characteristics of being able to retain its shape over time, thus ensuring years of use.

MAHINA

The grained texture makes this leather resilient up to a point but soft-to-the-touch Mahina is also vulnerable to marks and scuffs. Mahina goods require care and storage in proper dust bags when not being used. Neither is Mahina leather water resistant. The speciality Louis Vuitton design on Mahina goods are the perforations outlining the monogram print.

LOUIS VUITTON LUXURY LEATHERS

VERNIS LEATHER

'Vernis,' meaning varnish or 'sparkly' in French, is Louis Vuitton's monogram-embossed coated calfskin leather. Launched in 1998 by Marc Jacobs, then Artistic Director, it was introduced as a new twist on the brand's classic monogram pattern. Glossy and shiny, Vernis looks like patent leather but scratches and marks easily in addition to absorbing ink transfers – ie, it may pick up print or colours from newspapers.

TAURILLON

Top quality and butter-like to the touch, full-grained cowhide Taurillon leather is well known for Louis Vuitton's 'Capucine' line. Understated and minimalist in appearance, Taurillon is lightweight and extremely versatile.

TAIGA

Taiga leather has a corrected grain, meaning that any imperfections are sanded and buffed away before being printed with a new fine-yet-durable grain. Introduced into the House of Vuitton in the early 1990s, Taiga is mainly used for men's small leather goods such as cardholders, belts, wallets and briefcases.

THE FASHION ICONS — LOUIS VUITTON

BY GEORGES!

'Beware of Spurious Imitations'
Warning on an 1890s Louis Vuitton advertisement.

Born on July 13 1857, Georges Ferréol Vuitton was the only son of Louis and Clemence-Emilie. It was fortunate for the brand that Georges was passionate about the business from a young age. From childhood, he would walk around the corridors of the Asnières workshop where the workers called him 'Monsieur Georges', just as they called his father 'Monsieur Louis'. As a young teen, he was sent to school in the Channel Islands in order to become proficient in the English language. After two years he returned to Paris, his father believing two years of study were sufficient and that the boy would be best served working for the family firm. In January 1873, Georges officially became an apprentice at the Asnières workshops, successively learning the trades of packer, joiner, seller, delivery man and cashing agent, in addition to becoming familiar with the tools of the trade – the smoothing plane, the jack plane and the rasp.

If Louis Vuitton built the first stones in the building of the Louis Vuitton company, it was Georges who was the innovator. He turned the business into a luxury brand, creating sophisticated items for travel enthusiasts and building the company into a global success. Georges, a craftsman turned entrepreneur, invented a new code on how to live a luxury experience and make his brand exclusive. He was also an excellent businessman. Here are some of his greatest creations, personal and professional... in addition to the aforementioned Tumbler lock.

ABOVE: The Tumbler lock
RIGHT: Georges with his wife Joséphine and their children Gaston-Louis, and twins Pierre and Jean

1883 The birth of his eldest son, following his marriage to Joséphine Patrelle in 1880. Named Gaston-Louis Vuitton, the boy would join the family company as an apprentice in 1898.

1889 The birth of twin sons, Pierre and Jean.

1893 Georges exhibits luggage at the Chicago World Fair. The only vendor of French travel accessories present, he sells out entirely. J.P Morgan and his family become valued clients and Georges is introduced to famed retailer, John Wanamaker.

1896 – LV Canvas

Due to the popularity of the brand, many counterfeit LV products appeared in France and were sold at much lower prices, reflecting their poor craftsmanship. In 1896, in response to counterfeiters, Georges created a complicated pattern that would cover his trunks and reduce counterfeits due to the difficulty in creating the pattern. This resulted in the creation of the LV monogram canvas, which was both a response to counterfeits and an homage to his father, Louis. The motif was – and continues to be - a repetition of geometric flowers, diamond shapes and quatrefoils, accompanied by the letters LV. It was the first time a designer had placed his brand so prominently on his products. Georges was not to know that his design would become one of the most famous in the world and become a key part of the brand's image. Despite its creation in 1896, it was not until 1905 that the patent for the LV monogram canvas was granted.

1897 – Car Truck

Like many forward thinking folk at the end of the 19th century, Georges Vuitton was passionate about automobiles. His interest became an essential feature of Louis Vuitton trunks and how the brand created and innovated. Georges realised trunks were being made without any thought as to how they would fit into a car. He wanted to change this, deciding that travellers should be able to travel in a car with the same amount of cargo they could take on a boat or a train. A sturdier, more space-efficient trunk was required. Georges' solution was to use new materials he had not previously employed, including a black waterproof cloth that coated every trunk to ensure durability. He also decided to bevel each closure of the trunk, ensuring that they would not be so susceptible to issues caused by rain and dust. Georges knew that car-friendly trunks needed to be stacked on top of each other in order to use space

ABOVE: Chicago World Fair, 1893
RIGHT: An 1880 trunk by Louis Vuitton and an 1880's French corset

BY GEORGES!

efficiently. Therefore, he revolutionised the creation of trunks by squaring all edges and making them with flat tops and bottoms, and thus perfect for stacking. Georges Vuitton also bought the chassis of an automobile so that he could create his own car. He commissioned the likes of car bodybuilders Labourdette, Rothschild and Jeantaud to create an automobile which he could then use to match and design his own car trunks. In the year 1897, he presented the first prototype of the new trunk that he created—the Car Trunk. He presented his prototype and ideas at multiple automobile trade shows.

THE FASHION ICONS LOUIS VUITTON

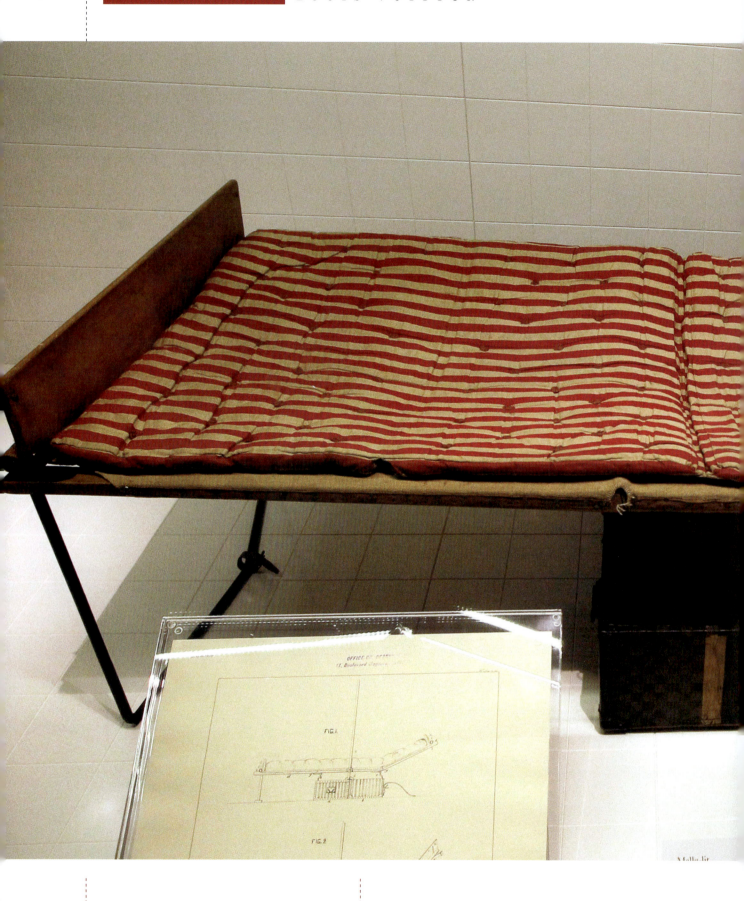

ABOVE: Malle lit, 1891

BY GEORGES! 23

1901 – The Steamer

Originally an essential on-board bag for travellers going on cruises, Georges introduced the Steamer, a trapezoidal-shaped travel bag with compartments to separate clean linen from that which had been worn. Until then, transatlantic travellers had had to make do with a linen bag and a separate night bag. The Steamer's unique shape would ultimately be the inspiration for the Alma bag.

1901 – Le Voyage

During George's tenure at the helm of Louis Vuitton, he began what is now a large part of Louis Vuitton's marketing - Le Voyage books. Georges created the first travel book published by Louis Vuitton, which has now turned into a 30-city collection of travel guides, including San Francisco, Hong Kong, Tokyo, Cape Town, Berlin and Amsterdam. A matching mobile app has also been created. Georges' book was published only in French in 1901 and centered on Paris, with three original editions existing each at a length of 294 pages.

1905 – The Perfect/Ideal Trunk

Initially named the 'Perfect' before being changed to the 'Ideal', this was a wardrobe in trunk form. With the dimensions of a large steamer trunk, two sides could be opened from the middle to the outside offering a global view of its interior. Fixed boxes in the chassis allowed smaller items to be stored.

1905 – 'Malle Lit'

Explorer Pierre Savorgnan de Brazza commissioned a 'Malle Lit' explorer's camp bed trunk in monogram canvas. Vuitton had previously developed a range of trunks covered in zinc, aluminium and copper designed for expeditions to the Tropics.

1906 – Vuitton et Fils

Eldest son and heir Gaston-Louis joins the management team, with Louis Vuitton becoming known as 'Vuitton et Fils.'

1908 – Aero Trunk

Georges Vuitton officially proposed a project for this lightweight, unsinkable trunk to support the creation of helicopter prototypes by his twin sons Jean and Pierre. Sadly, Jean passed away from a childhood illness a year later. His twin Pierre was killed while serving at the front in World War One.

ABOVE: The Steamer, 1901
TOP RIGHT: The Vuitton-Huber helicopter
BOTTOM RIGHT: A Louis Vuitton Flower Trunk

1908 – Gift Trunks

Rather than offering discounts, La Maison Vuitton chose to present loyal customers with mini Louis Vuitton trunks. These could not be bought or ordered but were gifts given at Georges' bequest and delivered to the client's home. The trunks were covered in the typical LV monogram canvas. Inside, Vuitton would place a bouquet of fresh flowers. The inside of the trunk contained a zinc tray so as to prevent any water or moisture damage from the flowers. Receiving these gifts was considered an honour as they were exclusive and could not be bought. After the flowers died, Georges allowed the recipient of the gift to choose how the trunk should be recycled—whether it be for sewing materials or as a cigarette box. Louis Vuitton no longer practices this custom. Flower trunks, however, are still available as part of their hard-sided collection.

THE FASHION ICONS | LOUIS VUITTON

ABOVE: Louis Vuitton's flagship store, Paris
RIGHT: Coco Chanel and the 'Alma' bag

1914 – Flagship Store

Georges moves the LV store to larger premises at 70 Champs-Élysées. The seven storey, early Art Deco building is the largest travel goods store in the world. Gaston-Louis takes charge, with his inspired window displays becoming the talk of Paris.

1915 – Chanel meets Vuitton

Georges was commissioned by Coco Chanel to make her a handbag in 1915. He subsequently produced a bespoke version of what would become firstly the Squire bag and then the Alma. The bag was Louis Vuitton's first foray into the world of ladies' handbags or purses. Like the products created by the brand, Georges Vuitton who passed away in 1936, played an essential role in developing a sustainable mindset around the luxury strategy. He developed a new philosophy which would later be formalized in business schools as a 'luxury pricing strategy'. This is a standard set by the Louis Vuitton brand and still followed by luxury brands today – ie, never cut prices or offer discounts, never lower quality but rather raise prices as demand increases.

LV BAG LADIES

AUDREY HEPBURN
Breakfast at Tiffany's star Audrey Hepburn was snapped carrying the Louis Vuitton Speedy at Heathrow airport in 1966. The legendary actress had requested the brand produce a smaller version of the bag. Voila La Speedy 25!

JENNIFER ANISTON
For a LV party at the Louvre in 2017, Jennifer Aniston clasps a small Louis Vuitton clutch bag, launched three years earlier. Resembling a small trunk, the purse pays homage to the brand's luggage heritage.

TWIGGY
Iconic model Twiggy was originally photographed carrying a LV brown monogram classic for Vogue in 1966.

REBEL WILSON
Actress Rebel Wilson loves a colour clash and nowhere is that more apparent than in this 2022 shot, taken in California. She sports a sunshine yellow LV bag against a hot pink jumpsuit.

SARAH JESSICA PARKER
Style icon and Sex in the City star Sarah Jessica is photographed with the no-longer available Saumur 30 Messenger Bag in 2012. Time for a relaunch?

LV BAG LADIES

NICOLE KIDMAN
Dressed by LV at the 2015 Oscars, Kidman accessorises her floor-length, sequined gown with a signature white Petite Malle bag by the brand.

VOGUE WILLIAMS
Irish presenter Vogue rocks a trusty Louis Vuitton Speedy holdall. Perfect for the busy mum of three as she goes about her business.

ROSIE HUNTINGTON-WHITELEY
Model Rosie tops off a stylish monochrome look for Paris Fashion Week with a classic LV black tote bag.

MIRANDA KERR
The LV ambassador for the Pacific Chill fragrance campaign in 2023, Miranda owns a number of the brand's bags. Here, she complements her look with a Louis Vuitton grab bag in burnt orange.

ANNA WINTOUR
Fashion legend Anna Wintour carries a LV monogram print clutch bag at the premiere for the David Beckham documentary in 2023.

GEMMA CHAN
Clashing patterns win hands-down at Wimbledon. Actress Gemma Chan serves up a bold look by pairing her monogram design LV bag with a cute patterned dress.

BLAKE LIVELY
Another fan of yellow is actress Blake Lively, papped in the Big Apple rocking a lemony-striped crossbody LV bag which completes the 1970s vibe.

THE FASHION ICONS — LOUIS VUITTON

TAYLOR SWIFT

Tay-Tay took inspiration from the late Princess Diana in an oversized top and cycling shorts in October 2023 – the pop Queen of Style completed the look with a LV Camera Box bag.

NAOMI CAMPBELL

Attending the Louis Vuitton Menswear Spring/Summer show in June 2023, model Naomi Campbell wore a brown leather LV mini dress and jacket combo, combining this with a striking red and white monogram-print duffle bag.

PARIS HILTON

Snapped in 2021, socialite Paris Hilton sports a bag from the 2009 LV range when, under Marc Jacobs' watch, the House of Vuitton collaborated with graffiti artist Stephen Sprouse.

ALEXA CHUNG

Fashion icon, writer and presenter Alexa Chung juxtaposes a shimmery gold evening number with her Twisted Box Louis Vuitton bag for a London Fashion Week party in 2022.

REESE WITHERSPOON

Reese goes full-on Elle Woods, her famous 'Legally Blonde' character, with this LV Capucines bag in hot pink. Featuring a grab handle and a long strap, it's practical as well as uber-chic.

SIENNA MILLER

Oh Sienna! The oh-so-stylish actress pairs a checked coat with a LV Cannes bag at a Louis Vuitton show in 2019.

LV BAG LADIES

VENUS WILLIAMS

Tennis Champion Venus Williams sports a reimagined classic hat box bag, as inspired by the brand's travel heritage, at the Louis Vuitton men's fashion show in 2022.

LAVERNE COX

A stylish and sophisticated 'Orange is the New Black' star Laverne Cox carries a subtle version of the monogram-print bag. Perfect with her classic camel coat and classy loafers.

KENDALL JENNER

Model Kendall goes vintage with this colourful micro number from the early 00's Takashi Murakami x Louis Vuitton collaboration.

RIHANNA

The face of Pharrell Williams' first menswear campaign for Louis Vuitton in 2023, super-star Rihanna shows off her business savvy with the help of this briefcase-inspired, oversized Louis Vuitton clutch bag.

ELLE FANNING

Louis Vuitton do luxury luggage like no other brand – of course they do. For a classically chic airport look, actress Elle travelled with the Horizon 55 suitcase and a Speedy 35 city bag. The statement stripes and personalisation add that extra special LV touch.

KOURTNEY KARDASHIAN

Sister Kourtney Kardashian also loves a LV micro bag, but hers is in a more traditional brown monogram print.

JULIANNE MOORE
A true LV muse, actress Julianne is photographed wearing Vuitton and carrying Vuitton – a Valisette BB mini tote bag.

ALICIA VIKANDER
Louis Vuitton muse, actress Alicia Vikander adds a burst of glamour to her black and white outfit with this sparkly LV mini bag – the ultimate party purse.

CHLOË GRACE MORETZ
Actress Chloé Moretz is the epitome of Parisian chic as she's spotted at Charles-de-Gaulle airport in Paris with a classic LV suitcase. Her Louis Vuitton Pochette crossbody bag is the perfect travelling companion.

BEYONCÉ
There are just 24 of the Louis Vuitton Tribute Patchwork Bags – and one of them belongs to Mrs Carter.

LV BAG LADIES 33

THE FASHION ICONS — LOUIS VUITTON

GASTON-LOUIS

'I almost was born in a trunk!'
Gaston-Louis Vuitton on a French TV programme in 1961.

Born on 30 January 1883 at Asnières, Gaston-Louis Vuitton – known as Gaston - was a fragile child beset by bronchial problems. His formative years alternated between school and spa-cures. He was later to say that he'd never failed an exam because he'd never sat one! He was, however, a bookish child who enjoyed reading, writing and sketching. As he grew to adulthood, his interest in the arts grew and he developed a life-long passion for collecting. He was also deeply interested in all aspects of design. Gaston started his apprenticeship at the Asnières workshops in 1897 before moving into the LV store at Rue Scribe in 1899. He would remain here for eight years, showing an instinctive talent as a salesman. In 1906 - having married his first love, Renée Versillé who, in the course of time, would give him six children - his father invited him to become part of the LV management. Georges and Gaston became something of a dynamic duo with the son and heir assuming a leading role in the company. Like his father, Georges, Gaston was passionate about the family business but unlike Georges, he was an aesthete in addition to being a shrewd businessman.

While feeling immense pride at what his father and grandfather had achieved, Gaston had ambitions beyond making trunks, luggage and travel bags. Sensitive to reading, arts, gardening and photography, his artistic eye enabled him to create magnificent window displays for the Louis Vuitton boutiques – and in particular the flagship Champs Élysées store. The Asnières workshops were adapted accordingly and in 1914 Louis Vuitton officially became a 'manufacturer of trunks, leather goods, goldsmith products and travel items'. In the Louis Vuitton catalogues, luxury products multiplied and resembled, in their finery, works of art. Although father Georges continued to be involved in the business until his death in 1936, it was Gaston who was the driving creative force at Louis Vuitton and continued to be until his own passing in 1970. Here is the timeline of some of his greatest achievements...

ABOVE: A Damier trunk from the late 1800's
RIGHT: Invitation for the talk-dinner of Gaston Vuitton to the sellers of caskets, trunks and packers

D'après une étiquette adresse. — Coll. Gast.-L. VUITTON.

LE VIEUX PAPIER
SOCIÉTÉ ARCHÉOLOGIQUE, HISTORIQUE ET ARTISTIQUE

LUNDI 11 MAI 1936 (231ᵉ Dîner)

Potage argenté - Bouchée financière
Gigot rôti
Haricots panachés
Savarin Chantilly - Corbeille de fruits

Causerie de M. Gaston-L. VUITTON
COFFRETIERS, MALLETIERS, EMBALLEURS
d'après les Papiers commerciaux, Factures, Prospectus, Cartes adresse

HOTEL DES EMPEREURS, 20, rue Jean-Jacques-Rousseau, Paris.

THE EARLY 1920s

An early devotee of Art Deco, Gaston collaborated with a number of fellow creatives as LV travel cases evolved. These featured exquisite miniature glass bottles by master craftsman René Lalique and silver items by silversmith and sculptor Jean Puiforcat. Gaston also started designing uber stylish dressing table accessories during this time.

1924

LV provides luggage for La Crociera Nera, an expedition organised by Citroën from Paris to Timbuktu.

1925

Gaston designs the company's stand at the Exposition Internationale des Arts Décoratifs et Industriels Modernes, Paris. It is difficult to overstate the impact this event had on the Art Deco movement, with the Vuitton display featuring a tortoise-shell fitted dressing case made for French Soprano Marthe Chenal in crocodile skin. World-famous opera singer Lily Pons ordered a special trunk to carry 36 pairs of shoes – six pairs more than usual as her feet were so small. The trunk's design still bears her name today.

TOP: Réne Lalique
ABOVE: An early 1920's advertisment
RIGHT: A shoe trunk

1927

In 1927, at the height of the glamorous Roaring Twenties, Gaston launched LV's very first fragrance. 'Heures d'Absence' was exclusive - there were just 300 bottles made and each was decorated with a miniature airplane motif to showcase the brand's enduring love of travel and adventure during the golden era of aviation.

1928

The Indian Maharajas became important clients of Vuitton, their love and understanding of craftsmanship leading them to place enormous orders. Picnic and dressing sets with silver fittings, cases for polo and fishing equipment, and a shoe polishing kit were commissioned by Hari Singh, Maharaja of Jammu and Kashmir.

1930

A big year for Gaston's LV with the introduction of the 'Keepall', a prototype of the modern holdall which is still in production to this day, and the 'Speedy' bag. Initially called the 'Express', the first model was available in a 30cm size, a more practical alternative to other, more capacious Vuitton designs of that time. As demand grew, the brand expanded the range, introducing 35cm and 40cm versions. During the 1960s, film star Audrey Hepburn made a special request for a smaller version of the bag, resulting in the exclusive creation of the 'Speedy 25'. Hepburn's petite 25cm style became a hit, and retains its trophy bag status to this day. Now, the Speedy comes in an assortment of iterations, and is permanently in demand on the resale market as vintage fashion becomes ever more popular. 1930 was also the year that Citroën's La Croisière Jaune expedition from Paris to Peking was furnished with Vuitton luggage.

LEFT: Louis Vuitton's first fragrance,
ABOVE: Audrey Hepburn at Rome airport

THE EARLY 1930s

The Exposition Coloniale Internationale opens in Paris, Vuitton's pavilion centred around a 20-foot high totem. Gaston-Louis' creations for the exhibition marry exotic skins and luxurious materials, each sourced from and inspired by the imperial colonies.

1932

During 1932, LV introduced the 'Noé' bag. Designed to transport up to five bottles of champagne and the response to a request from a champagne producer who needed an elegant way to carry the bottles. Noé has since become a popular and timeless staple known for its iconic bucket shape.

1934

With Coco Chanel's permission, LV started mass production of the design of her 1915 bag. Initially called the 'Squire', its name was changed to the 'Alma'. It quickly became one of Louis Vuitton's most popular pieces. The success of the Alma informed the brand's decision to diversify its product range by introducing smaller luxury goods.

1938

A visit to Paris by the British King George VI and his wife, Elizabeth, prompted LV to create a special gift to young Princesses Elizabeth and Margaret - a set of smooth cowhide suitcases, lined in pink moiré silk and crafted to house a pair of dolls.

1945

Gaston appointed eldest son, Henri-Louis, as business manager of Louis Vuitton.

1954

The centenary of Louis Vuitton. Loyal customers included Georges Simenon, the Duke and Duchess of Windsor, Christian Dior, Hubert de Givenchy, Charles Aznavour, Luchino Visconti and Kirk Douglas. This centennial year also saw LV HQ move from the overly touristy Champs Élysées to 78a Avenue Marceau - a more elegant address for customers who no longer liked the atmosphere of the Champs Élysées.

1959

Rubberised canvas was introduced, enabling LV to produce the first flexible luggage in monogram canvas.

1960s

A new influx of celebrities were photographed with Louis Vuitton goods including Brigitte Bardot, Alain Delon, Jackie Kennedy Onassis, Catherine Deneuve and David Bailey. It was during the 60s that the cylindrical Papillon handbag was launched.

Gaston-Louis Vuitton died in 1970. He continues to be known as 'the collector of objects' and for his love of delicate art which he injected not only into his life and hobbies, but also directly in the Louis Vuitton brand.

RIGHT: David Bailey and Catherine Deneuve at London Airport, 1966

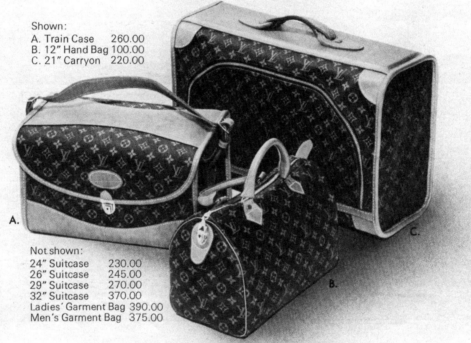

ABOVE: A 1960's USA Louis Vuitton magazine advert

CABINET OF WONDERS: THE GASTON-LOUIS VUITTON COLLECTION

'Gaston was a crazy collector of everything and anything. Thanks to him, we are starting to gather archives, with more than 100,000 documents, and 20,000 objects, not just from Louis Vuitton'

Benoit-Louis Vuitton, Gaston-Louis' great grandson.

In September 2017, some 47 years after Gaston-Louis' death, the House of Louis Vuitton published 'Cabinet of Wonders: The Gaston-Louis Vuitton Collection' – a luxury collation of images from Gaston-Louis' huge collection. A collector since his childhood, Gaston-Louis accumulated thousands of objects over his lifetime – much of which was spent in travel and discovery. His wide interests and voracious curiosity were intimately bound up with the future of the family business and with travel. In addition to forming his own collection of trunks – his primary motivation and the one he announced publicly – Gaston-Louis' roving eye lit upon rare antique travel articles, locks, hand tools, perfume bottles, tribal arts, walking sticks, vintage children's toys, books, hotel and travel labels, printed monograms and other typographical rarities. Together they form a rich personal evocation of curiosités industrielles, or curiosities of the trade, as he liked to call them. The fascinating assemblage – a melange of the strange and wonderful - offers an unprecedented insight into four key aspects in Gaston-Louis' life as a traveller, an inventor, a craftsman and an erudite.

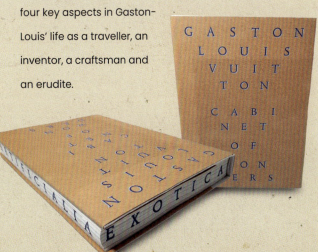

THE FASHION ICONS   LOUIS VUITTON

THE TOP TEN

Louis Vuitton's most iconic handbags. . .

The Speedy Bag

One of the most popular and recognizable bags of the Louis Vuitton brand, the Speedy was introduced in the 1930s and has since become one of the most iconic bags of all time. It is made of the brand's signature monogram canvas and features two leather handles and a zip closure. Available in different sizes, the iconic Speedy Bag was a particular favourite of the equally iconic Audrey Hepburn.

The Neverfull Bag

The Neverfull is another iconic handbag from the Louis Vuitton brand. The bag was first introduced in 2007 and has since become a favourite of many women worldwide. The bag is made of the brand's signature monogram canvas and features two leather handles and a drawstring closure. The Neverfull bag is available in different sizes and has been carried by celebrities such as Reese Witherspoon and Angelina Jolie.

The Alma Bag

The Alma bag is a classic LV handbag. Originally designed for Coco Chanel, the Alma was first introduced in the 1930s and has since become a universal favourite. Traditionally made from the brand's signature monogram canvas, it features a structured shape and leather handles. The Alma bag is available in different sizes and leathers, and has been carried by some of the world's most influential women, including Jacqueline Kennedy Onassis.

The Capucines Bag

The Capucines bag is a newer addition to the Louis Vuitton family of handbags. The bag was first introduced in 2013 and its name is an homage to the founder's first shop which was opened on Rue Neuve-des-Capucines in Paris in 1854. The bag is made of the brand's signature leather and features a structured shape and a top handle. The Capucines is available in different sizes and has been carried by celebrities such as Emma Stone and Miranda Kerr.

The Twist Bag

The Twist bag was first introduced in 2014 and has since become a favourite with celebrities such as Alicia Vikander and Michelle Williams. It features a twisting lock closure and chain strap. Available in several sizes.

The Petite Malle Bag

The Petite Malle bag is a unique and stylish handbag from LV. Launched in 2014, it is made of the brand's signature monogram canvas and features a structured shape and a top handle. The Petite Malle bag is available in different sizes and is a favourite with actresses Selena Gomez and Léa Seydoux.

The Noé Bag

The Noé bag is a true LV classic. Launched in 1932, it was originally a bespoke order for a champagne producer who wanted a stylish bag to accompany their bubbly. It was strategically designed to carry five bottles of champagne. The Noé, in LV's signature monogram canvas, features a drawstring closure and an adjustable shoulder strap. Rihanna and actress Sofía Vergara are fans.

The Pochette Accessoires Bag

The stylish and versatile Pochette Accessoires was introduced in the 1990s. Available in a range of sizes and the go-to purse for Kim Kardashian and Jennifer Lopez, it's made from the brand's signature monogram canvas and features a zip closure and a detachable shoulder strap.

The Artsy Bag

Unique and stylish, the Artsy bag – launched in 2010 - is a unique and stylish handbag from the Louis Vuitton brand, and features a slouchy shape and a single shoulder strap. The Artsy bag is available in different sizes and has been carried by celebrities such as Angelina Jolie and Kate Hudson.

The Keepall Bag

The Keepall bag is a classic travel bag from Louis Vuitton. The bag was first introduced in the 1930s and has since become one of the most renowned bags to date. Made of the brand's signature monogram canvas, it features two leather handles and a zip closure. The Keepall bag is available in different sizes and is a favourite with the rich and famous, including Kanye West and Pharrell Williams.

THE TOP TEN 45

ABOVE: The Damien Ebene canvas 'Alma BB' Bag

1970 - 1997

'The wolf in cashmere'

A description of Bernard Arnault who took over Louis Vuitton in 1989.

After his father's death in 1970, Henri-Louis Vuitton took over the running of Louis Vuitton. He was considered a safe pair of hands and held the high fashion fort until 1977 when he decided to retire. His brother-in-law Henri Racamier – married to Henri-Louis' sister Odile – became the man in charge. LV needed more than a safe pair of hands. Despite its popularity among the French elite, there were only two Louis Vuitton stores in France and sales volume was less than USD 10 million. Racamier, who was a self-made steel tycoon hailing from the Jura like the founder of the firm, is credited with placing Louis Vuitton on the world stage. He began to change the business model substantially, and turned the then still small leather goods shops into an international network of company operated shops worldwide to sell the merchandise. Within 10 years of Racamier taking charge, the Maison opened over 100 more stores globally – including several in France. In order to make the brand notable on an international scale, he started to sponsor top-of-the-range sporting events and created a new marketing strategy which would lead the brand to become better known worldwide.

ABOVE: Inside the Champs Élysées, Paris store
RIGHT: CEO Henri Racamier with his wife Odile Vuitton, circa 1989

1970 – 1997

In 1984, Racamier took Louis Vuitton public at the stock exchange. Three years later, LV - leader of high-end luggage, merged with Moët-Hennessy - king of champagne and cognac. At first, there was peace and harmony but before long, a kind of war broke out. Following different visions of the future of the Group, Alain Chevalier, the leader of Moët-Hennessy and Racamier, started to fight with the result that Racamier invited business wizard Bernard Arnault to invest in the company. The unhappy consequence of this was that, in 1989, Arnault managed to eject Racamier from the company board of Louis Vuitton. Racamier's plan had backfired and for the first time in its history, no family members were involved in the running of the business.

However, the 1990s saw Louis Vuitton truly go global as it began its gargantuan rise in the world of fashion. As a brand, Louis Vuitton embarked on its new exploration of the luxury fashion world and the contemporary dressing of an elite clientele. By the middle of the decade, Louis Vuitton was no longer viewed as the company who made luggage and bags favoured by women of a certain age. Expensive and well made, true, but also rather boring.

In 1996, Arnault began talking to hot, young designer Marc Jacobs. A year later, Jacobs and his long-time business partner Robert Duffy signed on as Artistic Director and Studio Director, respectively, of Louis Vuitton.

It truly was the dawning of a new age at LV.

ABOVE: President and Vice President of Louis Vuitton-Moët Hennessy (LVMH) Alain Chevalier (C) and Henri Racamier (L), Bernard Arnault (R), 1988

1970 – 1997

LOUIS VUITTON

ABOVE: Louis Vuitton magazine advert, 1990's

THE FASHION ICONS — LOUIS VUITTON

HAPPY HUNDREDTH!

In 1996, LV celebrated the centenary of the Monogram Canvas. To mark this momentous occasion, Louis Vuitton Paris invited some of the biggest names in fashion to present their interpretation of the company's 100-year history. Step forward Sybilla, Vivienne Westwood, Helmut Lang, Manolo Blahnik, Romeo Gigli, Azzedine Alaïa and Isaac Mizrahi.

RECORD CASE
Taking his cue from the trunk and luggage-making origins of the French brand, Austrian-born artist, Helmut Lang (pictured above), created a record bag – or rather case - that could hold up to 70 vinyls.

BUM BAG
British designer Vivienne Westwood (pictured left) collaborated with LV to design the Bum-Bag – inspired by bustle cages worn by women during the 1870s. This shape also appears in her designs from the mid-1990s.

HAPPY HUNDREDTH!

UMBRELLA BAG

Perhaps the boldest and most unusual piece from the brand's Monogram Centenaire collaboration, this backpack from iconic Spanish Designer Sybilla. Known for her outrageous and sculptural fashion creations, Sybilla's Umbrella Backpack features a built-in umbrella, perfect for going handsfree and staying dry while shopping.

SHOE BAG

Shoe-designer Manolo Blahnik's creation was – appropriately enough – a shoe bag in Monogram coated canvas with polished brass hardware, Vachetta leather trim, two flip lock closures at bottom, two flip lock closures, Louis Vuitton stamped S-lock closure at top and two round leather top handles. The interior was lined with fuchsia pink fabric with a zipper pocket and attached wire divider. The bag/trunk contained two removable drawstring shoe pouches and a large removable fabric pouch.

ALAÏA'S ALMA

Azzedine Alaïa's take on the iconic Alma handbag featured leopard calf hair over Louis Vuitton's iconic LV monogram logo coated canvas. The single knotted strap handle made it suitable for sliding over the arm and wearing at the elbow. AA's 'Alma' featured top zipper closure and was lined in woven cotton with two inner pockets.

SAC WEEKEND

Whilst others opted to use the instantly-recognisable, iconic monogrammed canvas, Isaac Mizrahi embraced a minimalist and fashion-forward aesthetic, removing the 'LV' almost entirely, with only a discreetly-stamped badge visible to the exterior.

HAPPY HUNDREDTH! 53

AMERICAN FOOTBALL BAG

Due to its unique shape – a pointed bottom and drawstring belt closure - Romeo Gigli's creation became known as the American football bag, although it was apparently inspired by flower baskets. It could be carried on the shoulder like a single strap backpack or also across the body.

THE FASHION ICONS   LOUIS VUITTON

THE MARC JACOBS YEARS

'This Vuitton thing was scary ... Suddenly you're on the Paris stage, with this huge name. I felt so paralyzed by it. That first collection was a no-win situation. I thought, if I give them what they expect, they'll be disappointed because they wanted to be surprised. If I give them a surprise, they'll be disappointed because it wasn't what they were expecting'

Marc Jacobs.

So, in 1997, maverick yet highly regarded designer Marc Jacobs was made Creative Director of Louis Vuitton. Having already created his own label, Jacobs was seen as the right person to modernise the brand. A shot in the arm, if you will. It turned out to be a genius decision.

Born in 1963 in New York, Jacobs was brought up by his paternal grandmother who initiated him when still a child into the world of fabrics and fashion, sewing and knitting. Clearly talented, he developed a passion for his craft which led him to attending the High School of Art and Design, and continuing on to enter the prestigious Parsons School of Design whilst working as a storekeeper in Charivari, an avant-garde concept store on the Upper West Side.

ABOVE: Marc Jacobs in his design studio, NY, 1989
RIGHT: Marc Jacobs' iconic grunge collection for Perry Ellis featuring model Christy Turlington

THE MARC JACOBS YEARS

In 1988 he was appointed Artistic Director of the American brand Perry Ellis where, having politely produced several 'respectably elegant' collections as expected, Jacobs paid homage to Seattle's grunge scene with his mismatched granny-dresses, flannel shirts and heavy Doctor Marten boots with his 1992 'grunge' collection. Supermodels Naomi Campbell, Christy Turlington, Kate Moss and Linda Evangelista were so into the collection, they agreed to walk in his show for free. However, 'grunge' was definitely not for Perry Ellis and Jacob was promptly fired. But he had bigger fashion fish to fry. Anna Wintour became a champion, publishing in his favour a fashion series entitled Grunge & Glory in US Vogue. That same year, 1993, he won his first Womenswear Designer of the Year award from the Council of Fashion Designers of America (CFDA) and became known as the 'Guru of Grunge'. He was the hottest designer in fashion – and LV needed to bask in his heat.

Under alternately 'grunge' and arty influences, Jacobs infused the brand with a touch of creative craziness. He launched LV's first ever women and men's collections and also its first jewellery range, based on a collection of charms.

Here are the highlights of King Marc's 16-year reign at LV...

THE LOGO

When he was hired, Jacobs was told he had a free hand, but that the logo must not be changed. But . . that's exactly what he did. 'Anti-snob snobbism' is Jacobs' 2001 work with designer Stephen Sprouse. In it, Sprouse and Jacobs translated the iconic LV logo into the urban, street, countercultural aesthetic. They launched a new model of the global brand and turned fashion-art collaborations into the backbone of the brand's relevance. Sprouse also collaborated with Jacobs in 2006 with a graffiti-style print for LV.

ABOVE: The new graffiti-style print

THE MARC JACOBS YEARS

MARC AND MURAKAMI

Jacobs collaborated with Takashi Murakami, a leading figure in the Japanese art world, in 2003. Murakami's illustrations covered Vuitton classics in candy colours, much favoured by the likes of Paris Hilton.

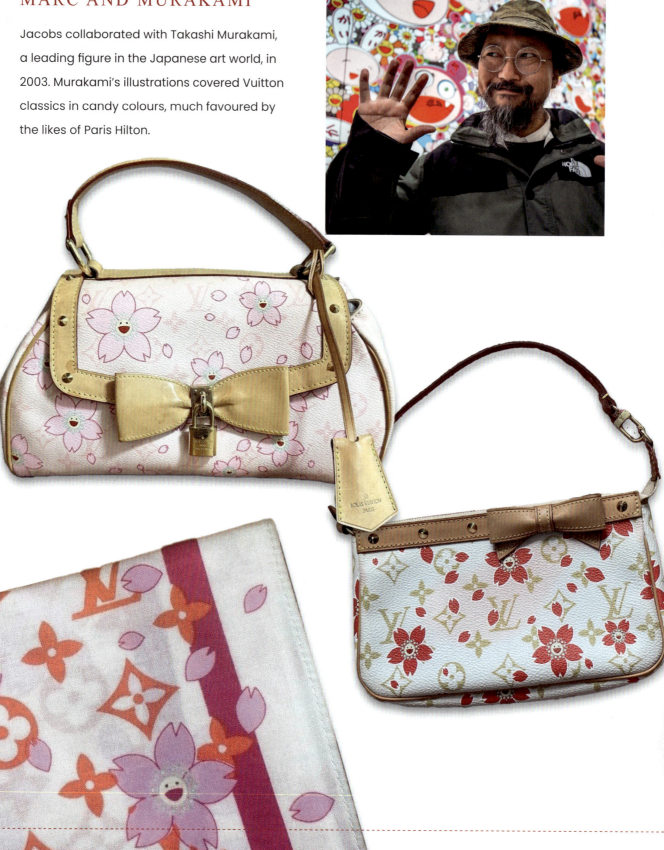

THE MARC JACOBS YEARS

NAUGHTY NURSES

In 2007, Jacobs and artist Richard Prince collaborated to come up with this kinky nurse inspired collection.

LEFT: Takashi Murakami and his collection
TOP: Collaboration with Richard Prince - A Jaune Denim Defile Weekender PM Pulp Bag
ABOVE: Spring/Summer RTW Collection, Paris

THE FASHION ICONS | LOUIS VUITTON

BIKER MESSENGER AFROS

If Paris was always on Jacobs' mood board, so too was his hometown of New York. The bike messengers that flooded the city appeared on the catwalk – with giant afro hairdos – in 2009.

THE MARC JACOBS YEARS

BUNNY EARS

Cutesy isn't a word associated with luxury high fashion, but Jacobs mischievous spirit came through in these high-fashion bunny ears. He wore them himself off the catwalk, as did Madonna.

LEFT: Paris Fashion Week Spring/Summer 2010
ABOVE: Fall/Winter 2009/2010 fashion show during Paris Fashion Week

AND GOD CREATED WOMAN ...

Jacobs never shied away from controversy. This collection came hot on the heels of the plus-size controversy. Celebrating feminine curves, he namechecked the classic va-va voom of Brigitte Bardot.

ABOVE: Paris Fashion Week Fall/Winter 2009/2010
RIGHT: Paris Fashion Week Fall/Winter 2012

THE NIGHT PORTER

Sex was never far away from Jacobs' LV collections. This 2011 show referenced the 1974's fetish-tinged movie, The Night Porter. Supermodels came down in lifts and carried whips.

THE FASHION ICONS | LOUIS VUITTON

ABOVE: Marc Jacobs at the end of his Spring/Summer RTW collection for LV in 2011, Paris

THE FASHION ICONS LOUIS VUITTON

MOSS ON A CAROUSEL

A supermodel in a dress of delicious marabou lightness is irresistible – especially when she's on a carousel as was Kate Moss in 2011.

ABOVE: Kate Moss walks the runway at the Spring/Summer show, 2011
RIGHT: Artist Kusama and an Infinity Dots lock it tote bag

JACOBS PLUS YAYOI KUSAMA

While at LV, Jacobs was the king of the collaboration. In 2012, he worked with Japanese artist Kusama on prints and bags, bringing her name – and trademark dots – to a global audience.

ABOVE: Paris Fashion Week Spring/Summer 2013 Collection

THE MARC JACOBS YEARS

THE TRAIN

'I was thinking about travel, the heritage of Louis Vuitton and then the romance of travelling on a train' said Marc Jacobs in 2012, explaining where the notion came from to stage his Vuitton collection aboard a steam engine.

Vuitton's history as a Malletier (trunk-maker) played a primary role, but so did Downton Abbey and the golden age of train travel between the wars. There was also a major fashion antecedent: in 1998, John Galliano steered a steam train rebranded as the 'Diorient Express' onto a platform of the Gare d'Austerlitz to open his autumn/winter haute couture show. Jacobs' show space, the Cour Carrée du Louvre in Paris, was decked out to resemble a vaulted turn-of-the-century station. The Louis Vuitton locomotive - specially constructed to precise requirements by an in-house team overseen by Louis Vuitton's visual creative director Faye McLeod - pulled in a full four minutes late to the platform at the Louvre, disgorging 47 of the most glamorous travellers ever. Each model —well over seven feet tall in six-inch platform shoes and towering cloche hats by London milliner Stephen Jones – was accompanied by a diminutive porter toting elaborately embellished luggage.

ABOVE: Fall/Winter 2012/2013 Collection show

THE MARC JACOBS YEARS   71

72 THE FASHION ICONS LOUIS VUITTON

ABOVE AND LEFT: Fall/Winter 2012/13 Collection show

THE MARC JACOBS YEARS 73

THE FASHION ICONS LOUIS VUITTON

THE FINAL COLLECTION

For Jacobs' Spring/Summer 2014 collection – his last for LV - the backdrop was a 'greatest hits' style mash-up of famous Vuitton set-pieces, including a little piece of the Louis Vuitton Express. This time, it was that clock looming large, counting down, and chiming to celebrate the finale of Marc Jacobs' remarkable 16-year tenure at the house.

When news broke that Jacobs would be leaving his post as creative director at Louis Vuitton - ostensibly to work on his own, individual collection - the fashion world was shocked. During his 'reign' at the brand, the designer was responsible for a whole new Vuitton aesthetic, which skyrocketed handbag sales for the House. He was able to take historical codes à la maison and transform them in a fresh and modern way. Jacobs will forever remain known for his pop-art visuals and splashy graphics, which helped him make his mark at LV forever and left fans longing for bags from the Marc Jacobs era well past his departure. A large part of the massive growth experienced by the House can be attributed to Jacobs' time at the LV helm.

ABOVE: Paris Fashion Week Spring/Summer 2014 show

THE MARC JACOBS YEARS

THE FASHION ICONS | LOUIS VUITTON

THE MARC JACOBS YEARS   77

LEFT: Paris Fashion Week Spring/Summer 2014 show'
ABOVE: Marc Jacobs taking his final bow as Creative Director for Louis Vuitton, 2014

THE FASHION ICONS LOUIS VUITTON

LV BY NUMBERS

1 — Louis Vuitton is the most valuable high fashion brand in the world

60 — the percentage of LV employees who are female

8 — the number of weeks Louis Vuitton takes for an internal order to be delivered

33,000 — the number of LV employees

460 — the number of Louis Vuitton stores around the world

4,000 — the number of leather goods specialists employed by Louis Vuitton

1997 — the year designer Marc Jacobs became creative director and came up with Louis Vuitton's first ready-to-wear clothing line

LV BY NUMBERS

2
LV releases a new runway collection of handbags twice a year

67,000
the price, in UK pounds, of the LV table tennis table

26.3 BN
in US dollars, the value of the Louis Vuitton brand in 2023

18
the number of LV workshops in France

17
the years that founder Louis Vuitton worked for Monsieur Mareshel before setting up his own company

3
the number of workshops in Italy, including a shoe factory

46
the number of perfumes in the LV fragrance base.

7
the number of days it takes to make one handbag

90,500
the number of searches per month on Google for the LV Neverfull bag

3
the generations of the Vuitton family who have run the brand

2023
the year Louis Vuitton launched its first baby collection

ST NICOLAS

'Louis Vuitton has always incarnated for me the symbol of ultimate luxury, innovation and exploration.'
Nicolas Ghesquière.

Nicolas Ghesquière, one of the most forward-thinking fashion designers in the world, took the reins as the new artistic director of women's collections at Louis Vuitton in November 2013. Ghesquière was appointed to re-energise and re-elevate LV into an uber luxury brand – something he has succeeded in doing.

Before Vuitton, Ghesquière spent a total of 15 years at Balenciaga, once an ailing womenswear house which he transformed into one of the most forward-thinking luxury brands in the world with his complex vision, sculptural tailoring and use of ultra-modern fabrics. Born in 1971 in Comines on the French/Belgian border and raised in the small town of Loudun in western France, Ghesquière announced at the age of 12 that he wanted to be a fashion designer. At 14, he secured an internship with French designer Agnès B for which he was paid in clothes. He worked from 1990 to 1992 as an assistant to designer Jean-Paul Gaultier. He then worked at Pôles, designing their knitwear line followed by a series of assignments with different companies including the Italian house of Callaghan.

In 2001, the same year that Ghesquière was named Womenswear Designer of the Year by the CFDA (Council of Fashion Designers of America), the Gucci Group bought Balenciaga, a move that Ghesquière welcomed.

'It is a happy relationship, it has worked because they want me to explain what I wanted to do with Balenciaga, not the other way around.'
Nicolas Ghesquière

RIGHT: Nicolas Ghesquière arriving at the Spring/Summer 2019 Paris Fashion Week

ST NICOLAS 81

THE FASHION ICONS   LOUIS VUITTON

Things later soured with Gucci Group's owners PPR (now Kering), and in November 2012, Ghesquière and PPR parted ways in what was said to be an acrimonious 'divorce'.

On November 4 2013, Ghesquière was announced as Louis Vuitton's new artistic director — just weeks after Marc Jacobs had announced his departure from the house.

'Louis Vuitton has always incarnated for me the symbol of ultimate luxury, innovation and exploration,' Ghesquière announced. 'I am very honoured of the mission that I am entrusted with, and proud to join the

ABOVE (L-R): Bernard Arnault, his wife Helene, Nicolas Ghesquière, Kim Jones, Delphine Arnault and Michael Burke

ST NICOLAS

history of this great Maison. We share common values and a vision.'

In keeping with Louis Vuitton's reputation of master bag-maker, Ghesquière's inimitable eye has forged the creation of many era-defining handbags. Namely, the sturdy, boxy Petite Malle bag - his first for Louis Vuitton - and the quilted leather GO-14 bag, inspired by his debut collection. But it is Ghesquière's theatrical extravaganzas presented at Paris Fashion Week and his wanderlust-inducing cruise collections that define him best as a designer. Here are some of the highlights of his career at LV thus far. . .

THE FASHION ICONS — LOUIS VUITTON

THE FIRST COLLECTION

Ghesquière's first ad campaign in Autumn/Winter 2014.

Ghesquière's opening collection at Vuitton for Fall/Winter 2014, entitled 'A New Day' was exactly that. The designer's debut, putting forth an entirely new spin on the historic house's DNA, silenced any doubters. Nicolas marked the start of his LV career with a bold collection that featured sleek leathers, belted jackets, A-line forms and a 70s tribute-meets-sports luxe. He combined colours and fabric into novelty pieces that were designed to symbolise the timeless sophistication of LV yet also signpost towards the future.

ABOVE & RIGHT: Ghesquière's opening collection at Vuitton for Autumn/WInter 2014

THE FASHION ICONS   LOUIS VUITTON

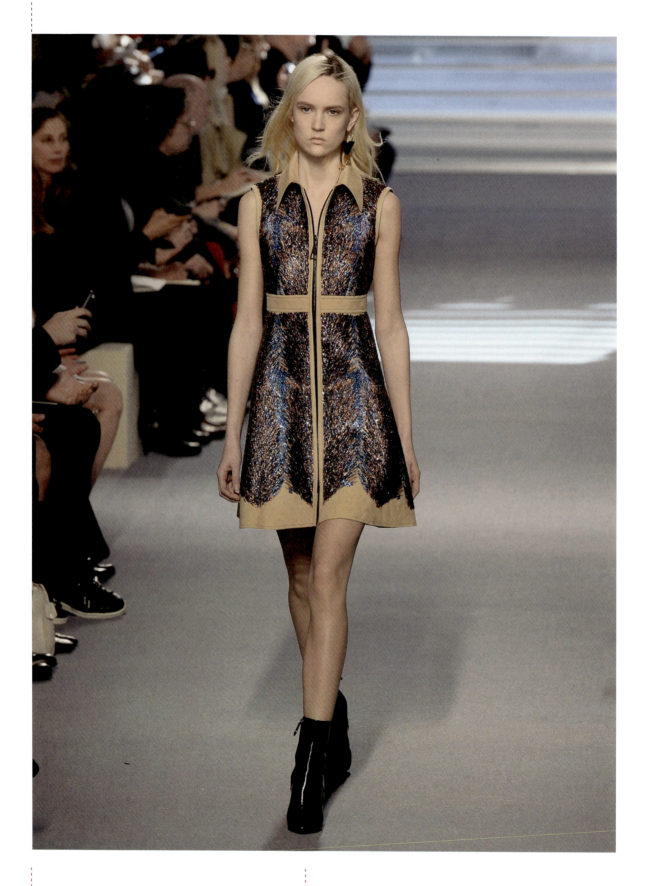

ABOVE & RIGHT: Ghesquière's opening collection at Vuitton for Autumn/WInter 2014

THE FASHION ICONS   LOUIS VUITTON

THE GO-14

Ghesquière introduced the GO-14 (named after its year of inception), incorporating the padded lambskin malletage, formerly reserved for the inside of a trunk, as a design element on its own.

THE PETITE MALLE

The Petite Malle was also a 2014 arrival, first spotted on the Vuitton runway. Literally a mini-trunk, the Petite Malle handbag is almost like buying a piece of Vuitton's rich history. Since its release, Ghesquière has created and introduced many iterations of this popular mini trunk.

THE 160TH ANNIVERSARY OF LOUIS VUITTON

Despite the success of his collection, Ghesquière was faced with yet another daunting task in his first year on the job – to commemorate the Maison's 160th founding anniversary in style. With a little help from executive vice president Delphine Arnault, he enlisted six iconoclasts of fashion and the creative industries – Karl Lagerfeld of Chanel, Christian Louboutin, Rei Kawakubo of Comme des Garçons, architect Frank Gehry, artist and photographer Cindy Sherman, and industrial designer Marc Newson – to design their individual takes on the concept of 'Celebrating Monogram'.

ABOVE (L-R): Karl Lagerfeld, Christian Louboutin, Rei Kawakubo, Cindy Sherman, Frank Gehry and Marc Newson.

LAGERFELD

In celebration of LV's iconic Monogram canvas, Lagerfeld imagined an extravagant set of luggage and accessories for devotees of boxing. His Boxing Trunk was fitted with a signature punching bag and stand, while a separate suitcase, also in Monogram, held boxing gloves and a mat. With its capacious interior and removable shelving, the trunk could also serve as a travel closet.

LOUBOUTIN

The Louboutin shopping bag combined the iconic Louis Vuitton Monogram pattern with Christian Louboutin's distinctive style, incorporating feminine touches, such as bows and red detailing, characteristic of his designs.

REI KAWAKUBO

Rei Kawakubo of Comme des Garçons' design featured three large 'frayed asymmetric cut-outs,' better known as holes, on either side. The fabric insert – the same sort of drawstring dust bag traditionally used to store and protect the outside of an expensive tote rather than line the inside – prevented the bag's contents from spilling out.

FRANK GEHRY

Architect Frank Gehry gave the classic LV handbag a unique structural re-think with the Twisted Box – said to resemble, in miniature, the Gehry-designed Walt Disney Concert Hall in Los Angeles. In 2023 Gehry unveiled 11 limited-edition handbags for LV.

CINDY SHERMAN

American Cindy Sherman sought inspiration from vintage travel patches and stickers often found on used luggage, creating fresh and unique appliqués to create her camera messenger bag with top handle and detachable shoulder strap.

MARC NEWSON

Industrial designer Newson set out to create a truly functional object – a sculptural backpack. 'I wanted to explore the Monogram's functional qualities. If you go back to the reason why the Monogram canvas was invented, it's because it's durable and it's weatherproof. But I wanted it to be fun as well – I don't like when things take themselves too seriously.'

SPRING/SUMMER 2016: TO THE FRONTIERS OF THE DIGITAL ERA

Ever the experimentalist for SS16, Ghesquière was inspired by the world of Anime, referencing the popular series 'Evangelion,' as well as Wong Kar-Wai's cult classic, '2046'. Entitled 'A Journey to the Frontiers of the Digital Era', a line-up of models channelled warrior princesses from the distant lands of RPG video games.

ST NICOLAS

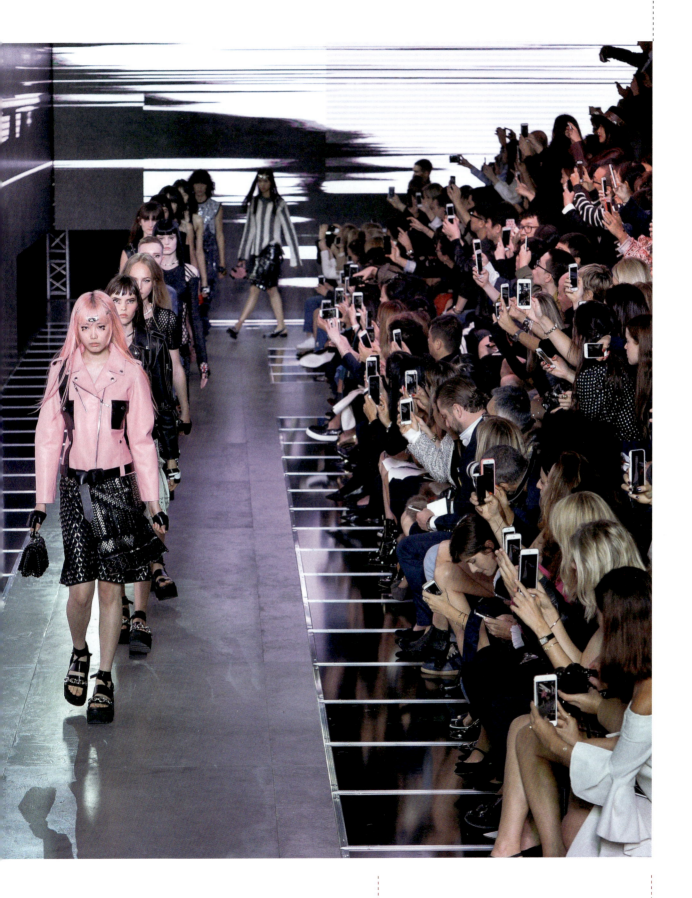

ABOVE: The Spring/Summer 2016 show

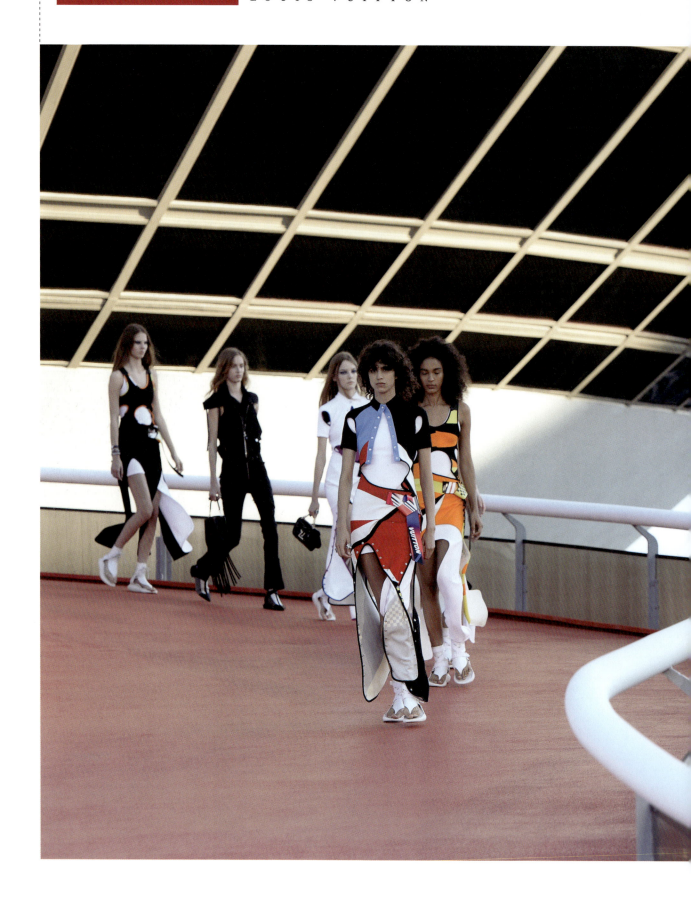

ST NICOLAS

ABOVE: The Cruise 2017 Collection Boombox bag
LEFT: The Cruise 2017 Collection in Niterói, Brazil

SPRING/SUMMER 2018: TRANSCENDING TIME

From back to the future and onto the past! For SS18, Ghesquière struck a striking balance between the sporty leggings, boxer shorts, and – for the first time in the brand's history – chunky-soled sneakers of modern-day athleisure.

Described as a vintage 1990s basketball and futuristic look, the chunky footwear and its oversized rubber sole with a technical mix of fabrics featured a unisex quality. Pairing suggestions include floral dresses and pops of colour blocks.

Ghesquière's obsession with Netflix's 'Stranger Things' was also clear to see in the spring 2018 womenswear show, where, to the delight of the audience, his salute to the show was a T-shirt tribute.

ST NICOLAS

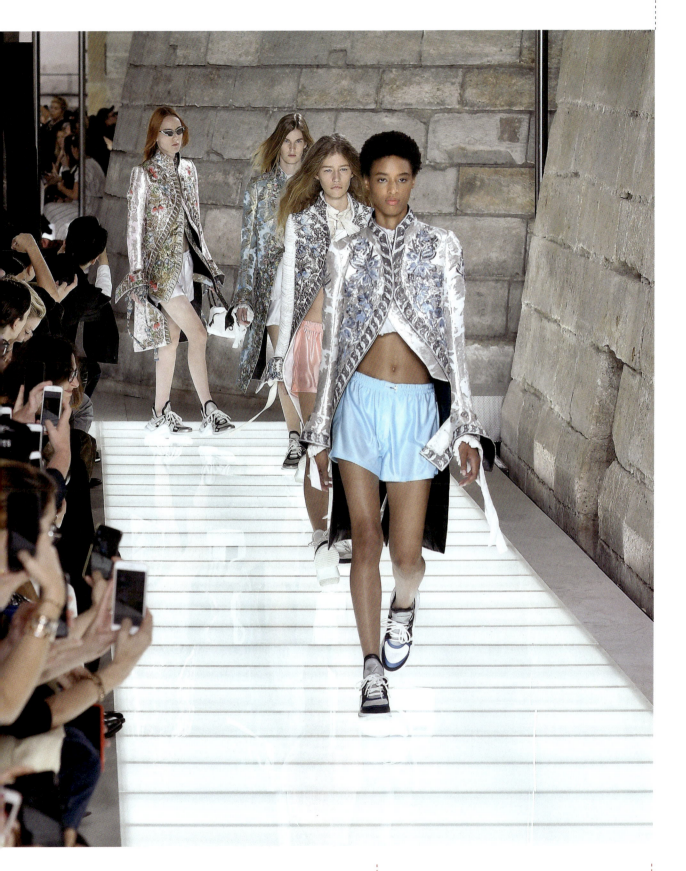

ABOVE: Models walking the SS18 show at Pyramide du Louvre in Paris
LEFT: Jacket detail from the SS18 show

THE FASHION ICONS — LOUIS VUITTON

FALL/WINTER 2020: ABOUT TIME

In addition to 2020 being the year COVID hit, it was also the year Ghesquière co-hosted the Costume Institute exhibition, christened 'About Time: Fashion and Duration'.

ST NICOLAS

The Fall runway was almost operatic, consisting of 200 chorus members outfitted in 400 years of fashion history – from the 15th century to the 1950s. The monogram jacquard 'Since 1854' collection also debuted in this show.

ABOVE: Nicolas Ghesquière walks on the runway at the Fall/Winter 2020/21 Fashion Week in Paris
LEFT: 'Since 1854' jacquard monogram

THE FASHION ICONS — LOUIS VUITTON

CRUISE 2021: GAME ON!

After a challenging 2020 for Cruise 2021, Ghesquière unveiled the 'Game On!' collection - with hearts, clubs, and spades motifs juxtaposed onto the classic multicolour monogram in popular, wearable styles - like the Speedy, the Neverfull, the Dauphine, and more.

ABOVE FROM THE TOP: Game On! The Speedy, Vanity PM, Neverfull, Dauphine and the Petite Malle bags
RIGHT: Emily Miller opening SS21

ST NICOLAS

SPRING/SUMMER 2021: WINGS OF DESIRE

Ahead of the year's presidential elections, Ghesquière's opening model for the SS21 runway model, Emily Miller, wore a knit sweater that simply read 'Vote'. More accessories followed, displaying his gender-inclusive ideals. Yet more surprises awaited on the bag front, where the launch of the new Coussin and the Rendez-vous bags created a cult-like buzz.

THE FASHION ICONS | LOUIS VUITTON

ABOVE & RIGHT: Models walk the runway at the opening of the Spring/Summer 2021 show

ST NICOLAS

THE FASHION ICONS   LOUIS VUITTON

CRUISE 2023: THE RETURN OF KUSAMA

Cruise 2023 saw the return of Vuitton-favourite Yayoi Kusama, whose technicolour polka dots had first taken the world by storm in the early 2010s. Kusama's Infinity Dots collection now encompassed a much wider range of purses, including monogram Empreinte and Epi styles!

ABOVE: Window display showcasing the Louis Vuitton X Yayoi Kusama collaboration
RIGHT: Display outside the Champs Élysées Store

10TH ANNIVERSARY SHOW

Exactly a decade to the day after he unveiled his first LV collection, on March 5 2024 Ghesquière staged his 10th Anniversary show in the central courtyard of the Louvre in Paris. It was a classic with few gimmicks or stunts, and the likes of 'A' listers Emma Stone and Zendaya were in situ to witness it. The show was utterly celebratory, described as an 'exploration of introspection' that 'bears witness to a decade of fashion'. Ghesquière was looking back as well as looking forward. The dresses that were printed with the iconography of LV luggage were very obviously throwbacks to the house's history, but over 10 years Ghesquière has made LV his own. Bomber jackets and panelled trousers featured bias cuts while Japanese-style wrap dresses were matched with leather hats and nearly every outfit was paired with a pair of furry gloves. With the myriad of styles and cuts in this collection, there was something in this anniversary collection for all women.

He prefers to say he 'builds' his collections, rather than designs them. And he sees his work as collage—a whole much bigger than any of its sundry singular parts. Ghesquière is known for his innovative designs and forward-thinking approach to fashion—and his time at Vuitton has simply allowed this talent to flower into some of the most iconoclastic collections that define our times. His talent for modernity is given a powerful boost by the innovative, high quality and state of the art materials and craftsmanship afforded by one of the world's foremost luxury houses.

'It's not about trying to create new [for the sake of being] new. It's about trying to find a new feeling with an already [existing] shape,'

Nicolas Ghesquière

RIGHT: Nicolas Ghesquière walks on the runway at the end of the show

THE FASHION ICONS | LOUIS VUITTON

ABOVE: Paris Fashion Week, Fall/Winter 24 Collection

THE FASHION ICONS | LOUIS VUITTON

ABOVE: Paris Fashion Week, Fall/Winter 24 Collection

ONLY AT LOUIS VUITTON

Sartorially special, universally unique...

✳ It's reported that a LV bag was the only item of luggage to survive the sinking of the Titanic in 1912. It sunk to the bottom of the ocean, however the bag were in a reasonable condition thanks to the superior waterproofing and seam-sealing.

✳ Louis Vuitton never has sales, choosing instead to keep products at fixed prices all year round. You won't find any Louis Vuitton outlet stores, and you won't see the company selling wholesale either. The brand warns its customers against buying heavily discounted bags online, which are often counterfeit goods.

✳ In 1927, American author Ernest Hemingway became the lucky owner of his own custom trunk designed by Gaston-Louis Vuitton. Hemingway's library trunk was a mish mash of shelves and secret drawers, no doubt housing his personal collection of books, and a compartment large enough to house his typewriter.

✳ In 2012, Louis Vuitton introduced the Haute Maroquinerie service. This offers the brand's top clients the opportunity to design their own bag based on preselected shapes, leathers and colours. Customers can pick from the five shapes pictured below in several sizes, eight types of ultra-premium leather (including crocodile) and more than 25 colours. The bags are then almost entirely handmade upon order to the customer's specifications, and the client's name is engraved on the interior of the bag. The Haute Maroquinerie design rooms are only available in select Maison stores which include flagships in Paris, Milan, New York, Sydney, Taipei, and London.

✳ The handles and piping of original LV bags are made of cow-hide leather which is a light tan colour, while the edge is dyed red with yellow stitching. After using the bag for a few weeks, the leather handle changes into dark brown. If it doesn't, then it's a fake.

* Louis Vuitton bags are half the price in France as they are in China, so a lot of Chinese shoppers buy them while on vacation in France.

* Among the various Louis Vuitton stores is the two-storey floating building in Singapore. It has state-of-the-art features, including an underwater access tunnel, a relaxation deck, and a bookstore.

* In 2011, Georgian artist Irakli Kiziria introduced Louis Vuitton monogram-bearing condoms on World Aids Day. The artist came up with this idea because LVMH (Louis Vuitton's parent company) supports various organizations in the field of public health research. Costing about 60 euros and packaged in the golden brown colours showing the distinctive characters of Louis Vuitton, a part of the sale proceeds were said to have been donated to charity. A noble idea, but its implementation was seen to damage the carefully constructed image of Louis Vuitton. The product no longer appears on the website of the artist.

* There is a Louis Vuitton teddy bear. Originally produced in 2000, the Steiff Louis Teddy Bear cost a whopping $2.1 million, making it the world's most expensive teddy bear. It was bought by Jessie Kim, a renowned Korean collector, and remains at the country's teddy bear museum.

* Even though they have trademarked their signature design, 99% of Louis Vuitton merchandise in the world is fake.

* LV bags are not delicate. Instead, each bag goes through several durability tests - it is dropped from a height of half a meter for 4 days straight with a weight of 3.5 kgs inside, among other endurance tests. The material undergoes a bombardment of ultraviolet rays to ensure resistance to fading. Also, the zippers are tugged open and shut around 5,000 times to ensure they work well while in the hands of a customer.

* At the end of the year, if any LV products are not sold, they are sent back to the LV factory in France where they are shredded or burnt. They take this drastic measure only to maintain the exclusivity of their brand.

The famous LV monogram inspired artist Salvador Dalí to create the 'Daligram'

 Mikhail Gorbachev, the last president of the USSR, once posed for a Louis Vuitton ad campaign.

 Known for creating luxury bags and accessories, Louis Vuitton once created a collection of luxury pens.

 To further personalise a LV trunk, artisans trained in Asnières offer hand-painting services. Clients may choose to have initials hot stamped on a luggage tag or stripes and initials or a family crest hand-painted on their commissioned trunk. This exclusive process begins with a private consultation and continues with further correspondence until the final design is approved. As the intricate hand-painting is ongoing—a process that can take about three months—the client advisor will send regular work-in-progress updates, to allow maximum involvement in this artistic endeavour.

 Hand-painting the Monogram canvas requires highly specialised skills. After sketching the design on the canvas, thin layers of specially formulated acrylic paint are slowly applied. Each layer has to be completely dry before another can be added and this process is repeated until the canvas is perfectly covered. The artisan also has to ensure the paint is not too thick, avoiding cracks or obvious bumps on the surface of the canvas.

 In the past, travel stickers functioned as a record of one's adventures around the globe. Gaston-Louis Vuitton was fascinated by these stickers and collected vintage travel labels, many of which were ultimately published in a book, 'Escales Autour Du Monde', by well-known travel writer, Francisca Mattéoli. In tribute to this charming heritage, Louis Vuitton has created a series of World Tour 'stickers' inspired by cities around the world. They include unique emblems for Paris, Tokyo, Shanghai, Miami and Singapore. Unlike conventional stickers which tear and age with time, these are hand-painted on trunks and luggage to provide an elegant and long-lasting record of one's global adventures.

ONLY AT LOUIS VUITTON

✱ While the trunks protect prized belongings, sometimes they also encase secrets and important documents from prying eyes. French explorer Pierre Savorgnan de Brazza ordered a Trunk Bed with a secret drawer in 1879, which he used while investigating conditions in French territories, including examples of forced labour, massacres and misappropriated funds. He kept these notes in the secret trunk drawer, determined to hand them safely back to the French government. It is said the drawer was so well concealed, Georges Vuitton had to be summoned to reopen it.

✱ Creative director Nicolas Ghesquière's highly coveted Petite Malle bag is a modern piece that cleverly pays homage to one of the maison's most iconic travellers - photographer and philanthropist Albert Kahn. From 1911 to 1929, the brand created several trunks for Kahn's expeditions with padded compartments to hold camera equipment. When Ghesquière reinvented the trunk for his debut autumn/winter 2014 collection, he kept the signature motif on the mini-trunk clutches in a nod to Kahn's spirit of adventure.

✱ In 2016, Louis Vuitton unveiled new product packaging in a bright saffron shade called 'Sarfran Imperial'. This replaced the former chocolate-brown coloured boxes, bags and gift-wrapping. The colour first appeared early in the history of the Maison, as featured in many iconic heritage pieces, in particular the 'Citroën' trunk made by Louis Vuitton for an expedition to Africa organized by the automaker in 1924.

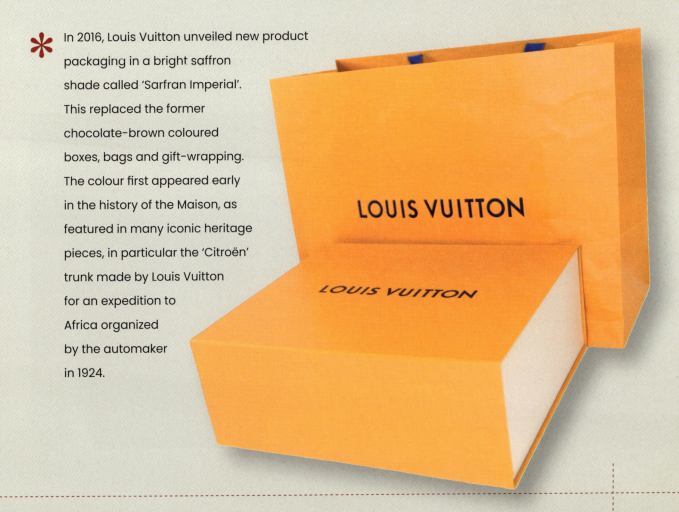

THE FASHION ICONS — LOUIS VUITTON

LOUIS VUITTON AND THE A LISTERS

'I am glad to welcome Pharrell back home, after our collaborations in 2004 and 2008 for Louis Vuitton, as our new Men's Creative Director. His creative vision beyond fashion will undoubtedly lead Louis Vuitton towards a new and very exciting chapter'

Pietro Beccari, Louis Vuitton's Chairman and CEO, February 2023.

LV's connections and collaborations with celebrities go way back. The brand's luxury luggage lines and leather goods have long been a hit with the world's most fashionable. As mentioned earlier, Coco Chanel carried Vuitton bags as did the Duke and Duchess of Windsor, who were great party-throwers and travelled with a wardrobe trunk. Audrey Hepburn, Jackie Kennedy Onassis, Catherine Deneuve and Lauren Bacall were just some of the legendary 20th-century stars who bought into the monogram. More recently, the brand is a go-to for the Kardashian clan, Sarah Jessica Parker, Beyonce, the Beckhams and the Hadids. However, some celebrities have gone beyond merely carrying Louis Vuitton items to becoming official faces of the brand. Madonna, Uma Thurman, Scarlett Johansson, the late Sean Connery and most recently Rihanna have all appeared in marketing campaigns for Louis Vuitton, further solidifying the connection between the luxury brand and Hollywood glamour.

RIGHT: U.S rapper Pharrell Williams attends the Louis Vuitton men's Fall/Winter 2008/2009 fashion collection, Paris

LOUIS VUITTON AND THE A LISTERS

As of 2023, there were thirteen A listers who were official House Ambassadors - J-Hope, Jung Ho-yeon, Liu Yifei, TaeYeon, Zendaya, Tahar Rahim, Hyein, Chloë Grace Moretz, Song Joong-ki, Cate Blanchett, Zhu Yilong, Jackson Wang and Carlos Alcaraz – with LV actively courting the growing markets of Asia and the Far East. Going into 2024 and looking forward to the Parisian Olympics, Vuitton turned their attention to the world of sports, 'signing up' French basketball player Victor Wembanyama, tennis players Carlos Alcaraz and Naomi Osaka, skier Eileen Gu, swimmer Léon Marchand and fencer Enzo Lefort, among others, to represent the house.

In addition to their brand ambassadors, Louis Vuitton is proud of its creative collaborations with A list actors and musicians. Think the Kanye West sneakers from 2009 and Millie Bobby Brown's 2024 Silver Lockit jewellery collection in support of UNICEF. The jewel in this particular part of the LV crown, however, is the input of Pharrell Williams, who was appointed Louis Vuitton's Men's Creative Director in February 2023, following the untimely death of his predecessor and friend Virgil Abloh. 'Renaissance Man' Pharrell's relationship with Louis Vuitton began in 2004, with the release of his "Millionaire" sunglasses in collaboration with Marc Jacobs and Nigo. The thick red aviators, with monogrammed

ABOVE: Zendaya, Cate Blanchett and the 1.1 Millionaires Sunglasses Exclusives

so that Abloh updated the glasses in 2018 as part of his initial LV show. In 2008, Pharrell worked with Louis Vuitton once again, collaborating on a jewellery line with Camille Miceli. The pieces were inventive and fantastical, with Pharrell's striking use of colour and flashy love of sparkle truly making the collection a work of art.

> *'This is the crown jewel of the LVMH portfolio. It's everything, and I was appointed to rule in this position,'* Pharrell said on his appointment. *'So No.1, a ruler of a position is usually like a king. But a ruler of this position for me is a perpetual student. It's what I intend to be.'*

The title of Louis Vuitton's Creative Director for Menswear is just another addition to Williams' legendary resume. First making his way into the entertainment industry as a music producer in the early 1990s, he rose to fame as one-half of The Neptunes (who have worked with just about every notable music act you can think of including the likes of Justin Timberlake and Jay-Z). Williams then started a solo career of his own with 2003's 'Frontin' and released his debut album 'In My Mind' in 2006. While Williams' musical accomplishments are endless, fashion is always something that's been a huge part of his career, creating his streetwear label Billionaire Boys Club in 2003. In 2014, Williams signed a deal with Adidas, making it the first time the brand had ever partnered with anybody who owned their own textile company. Then came the LV appointment. While we are still very early into the 'Happy' hit-maker's tenure, here are some of his standout creations thus far...

RIGHT: Pharrell's first Louis Vuitton show 2023/2024

SPRING SUMMER 2024

No fashion show in recent memory has grabbed more global headlines than Williams' first collection in June 2023. Taking place on an illuminated Pont Neuf, the oldest standing bridge crossing the River Seine in Paris, and before a star-studded crowd including Beyonce, Jay Z and Zendaya, Pharrell unveiled his vision. Using the house's signature 'Damier' check as a starting point, Williams riffed on the historic pattern, transforming it into pixelated, workwear-inspired garments. He titled it 'the Damouflage'. Williams said he was inspired by memories of his childhood at Princess Anne High School in Virginia to create inspired elements of American varsity wear - like a collegiate style jacket emblazoned with 'LV Lovers'. He also venerated the iconic LV trunk. In one memorable moment, a stack of monogrammed trunks was driven along the runway in the back of a military-style buggy. New versions of the Louis Vuitton 'Speedy' handbag were on show, the structured shape transformed by using soft leather with Williams saying he wanted the bag to reflect real-life needs and thus collapsing and draping to the wearer's body.

PRE-FALL COLLECTION 2024

The next stage of Williams' LV vision was revealed on a Thursday evening in December 2023 in Hong Kong's Victoria Harbour. Twelve hundred guests packed into the waterside Avenue of Stars, HK's version of Hollywood's Walk of Fame. There was a definite holiday vibe with sand covering the runway and ukulele music floating in the air. In the show, American streetwear with European tailoring was juxtaposed with Japanese workwear. When he took the job, Pharrell said he was designing for himself, because he was a prime Louis Vuitton customer and his personal 'dandy' style came through in this collection – from the two-tone suede loafers, shiny off-white suit with flared trousers that opened the show to soft chambray suits, mariner's jackets buttoned with pearls, and jaunty sailors' hats. Surf-themed fashion was also on show with avidly vivid tropical prints covering suits, sets and piles of bags.

ABOVE: The Louis Vuitton pre-fall 2024 men's collection at the Avenue of Stars promenade in Hong Kong, China.

LOUIS VUITTON AND THE A LISTERS

THE FASHION ICONS | LOUIS VUITTON

ABOVE & RIGHT: Models walk the runway in a design by Pharrell Williams during the Louis Vuitton Men's Pre-Fall 2024 fashion show

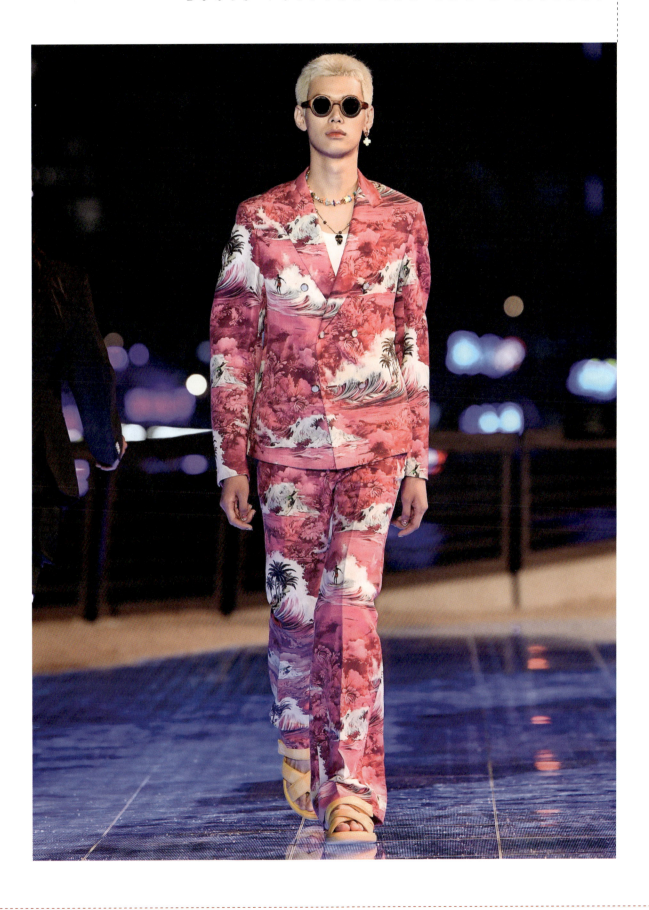

FALL/WINTER 2024

For Louis Vuitton's Fall/Winter 2024 collection, designer Pharrell Williams brought the American West to Paris. Presenting an 80-look collection filled with boots, bags, hats, and jackets—a spirit of classic Americana shown to a soundtrack of creative collaborations and new music from artists like Mumford & Sons. There were cowboy shirts, chaps and workwear silhouettes enriched by details like turquoise beading. The set was AI-designed and reminiscent of Colorado's Monument Valley. The collection included a collaboration with the American bootmaker Timberland, which the designer had teased on his unofficial Instagram account a few days before. The collaboration consisted of 10 different designs of the typical Timberland work boots, including a limited-edition boot crafted with eyelets and tongue pendants featuring the LV monogram.

ABOVE: Designed by Pharrell Williams, Louis Vuitton Men's Fall/Winter 2024 fashion show

THE FASHION ICONS LOUIS VUITTON

ABOVE: Pharrell Williams walks the runway at the end of his show

SPRING/SUMMER 2025

Pharrell Williams' fourth show as creative director of menswear at Louis Vuitton took place in the flag-lined gardens of the Unesco building in Paris, June 2024. The emphasis of the show was the international nature of the location, and the importance of diversity. Once the show began, however, a theme emerged that was perhaps more front of mind for those who were in Paris in June '24 – ie, the Olympics and the Euros. There were sporting references throughout, especially to football. Some models wore shirts with 'LVFC' written across them, while one had a bag shaped like a football, covered in the famous LV monogram. Another had a jacket referencing motocross. For Williams the theme went beyond sport. '[It is] the celebration of human athletic prowess,' he said. '[We are] just committed to that notion [to] show the world how beautiful we are as a species from the Blackest of the Black to the whitest of the white.' This message came through in the casting of the show and how the models' outfits were designed to match with their different skin tones.

Ultimately, Williams said, the show was designed to be 'about unity and the oneness of what one could look like when you just invite everybody in as a whole. We are appreciative of this opportunity and this platform that is at Louis Vuitton.'

ABOVE & RIGHT: Spring/Summer 2025 fashion show as part of the Paris Men Fashion Week

LOUIS VUITTON AND THE A LISTERS 131

THE FASHION ICONS | LOUIS VUITTON

ABOVE & RIGHT: Spring/Summer 2025 fashion show as part of the Paris Men Fashion Week

PARIS OLYMPICS 2024

LVMH immediately took the Paris Olympics by storm, with Pharrell Williams himself taking centre stage and igniting the Games with unparalleled flair. As he carried the Olympic torch to the Basilica of Saint-Denis, his Louis Vuitton ensemble turned the event into a high-fashion spectacle, balancing elegance with sleek athletic functionality. But this was not the first stamp of Louis Vuitton witnessed by the Paris Games, as a couple of months earlier in May, the iconic Belem ship carrying the Olympic flame docked in Marseille, and presented the torch from a custom Louis Vuitton Damier trunk - the torch trunk. As part of LVMH's high-profile sponsorship, Berluti crafted the French Olympic team's uniforms, while Pharrell's Louis Vuitton-designed uniforms and salvers were used for presenting the awards. Louis Vuitton's extensive participation in the 2024 Olympics illuminates its deep, unbreakable bond with Paris, and showcased Pharrell's ability to push the brand further into the energetic and vibrant world of sport.

ABOVE: Olympic rings on the Eiffel Tower

LOUIS VUITTON AND THE A LISTERS 135

ABOVE: Pharrell Williams stands next to the custom-designed trunk containing the Olympic torch as part of the 2024 Paris Olympic Games

SAY WHAT?
Talking up LV

Reality star Kim Kardashian
"There's a lot of baggage that comes along with our family, but it's like Louis Vuitton baggage."

Rapper and singer Nicki Minaj
"I don't put cash in my Louis Vuitton wallet. I have it thrown around my bag - just a whole bunch of hundreds, maybe $5,000."

Actor Luke Evans
"Good suits don't come from anywhere, though - I mainly wear Armani, Louis Vuitton and Burberry."

Artist, rapper and singer/songwriter Pharrell Williams
"Working at LV? This is not a job. This is not a gig. This is a dream."

Media legend and actress Oprah Winfrey

"I used to have a fake Louis Vuitton bag because I thought it meant something in life. But now I realize that all the things in the world don't define you. It's what you stand for, what you're willing to do, how close to the truth you're willing to be in your life."

Actress Reese Witherspoon

"I grew up in Tennessee. We didn't know what Louis Vuitton was. I had to order all my prom outfits out of catalogs."

Rapper and singer/songwriter Kanye West

"I thank Marc Jacobs so much for giving me the opportunity to design a shoe for Louis Vuitton, but the thing that broke my heart most was when they said, 'You're finished. The shoe's finished.

Keep rockin', and keep knockin' Whether you Louis Vuitton it up or Reebokin' You see the hate, that they're servin' on a platter. So what we gon' have, dessert or disaster?

I'm Kon the Louis Vuitton Don / Bought my Mom a purse now she Louis Vuitton Mom / Still might throw on a little low-on / They want me to stop, go on, go on / They don't want me to shop and me spending that hard / Oh my God, is that a black card? / I turned around and replied Why yes / But I prefer the term African American Express.

I know I've been called the Louis Vuitton Don ... I've been called a lot of names ... Due to what happened, so severely, when the red shoes hit the runway, I was forced to change my name to Martin Louis Vuitton the King, Jr. Address me as such."

Actress, writer and comedian Tina Fey

"Do I think Photoshop is being used excessively? Yes. I saw Madonna's Louis Vuitton ad and honestly, at first glance, I thought it was Gwen Stefani's baby."

Dutch model Rianne Van Rompaey

"I've met some of my best friends at Louis Vuitton. It's been a really important thread throughout my life."

Actress Zendaya

"I remember growing up around LV campaigns. There was this one that I loved from the early 2000s of Naomi Campbell, and she's like sprawled out over a trunk. I can still see it. I can see the image in my head and I remember seeing it in magazines as a kid. Everyone had the LV-print on their Myspace page."

Actress and LV muse Alicia Vikander

"I love the fact that fashion allows me to step into different personas and shoes and really push those boundaries, but LV just always makes everything still feel like me, she says, like an extended and bigger version of myself."

Reality star Jessica Simpson

"Is that weird, taking my Louis Vuitton bag camping?"

Actress Selena Gomez

"My first big career purchase when I was, like, 17 was a Louis Vuitton laptop bag. Now, seeing the exhibit [Louis Vuitton's "Series 3" exhibition in London], it's exciting because I feel like I kind of know it. It's weird - it's almost like something you grow up with and you just know a little bit about it. Now that I'm immersed in it, it's kind of insane."

Model and businesswoman Dita Von Teese

"Don't underestimate the cosmetic power of sunglasses. It's worth spending a bit of money on a quality pair. I usually go for Dior or Louis Vuitton."

Musician Danielle Haim

"We grew up dressing ourselves and going to thrift stores trying to recreate his looks, so when we found out Louis Vuitton was interested in working with us, it was like this holy grail."

Fashion model Liu Wen

"The first time at Louis Vuitton was Spring 2009 season, and I remember that the colors of the clothes were very dreamy."